PowerShell

A Comprehensive Guide to
Windows PowerShell

Table of Contents

Introduction

Are you looking for an easy way to simplify and automate administration of all your Microsoft products? You can't go wrong with Microsoft PowerShell, one of the most powerful scripting languages ever devised. And don't let the term, "scripting language" scare you off either; PowerShell is remarkably easy to learn and has one of the most comprehensive support systems of any programming or scripting language.

PowerShell makes it easy to retrieve data about your system settings, manage your services, change objects and much more; learning it now will help you to reduce how much time you have to spend, or waste as the case may be, on admin functions and all without the need to purchase expensive tools or services from elsewhere. It comes built into Windows 10, so you don't even have to go through the hassle of downloading and setting it up – it's all there, just waiting for you to use.

In this guide, we will cover:

- What PowerShell is and what its uses are
- PowerShell cmdlets (commands)
- PowerShell scripts
- PowerShell strings and quotes
- PowerShell Automation and PowerShell Remoting

Rather than having one underlying theme running through the book, I have set it out so that you can pick and choose the chapter you want to read, depending on your needs at the time.

Welcome to the wonders of Windows PowerShell.

Chapter 1: Introduction to PowerShell

Let's start with the basics – what is PowerShell and what can it do for you?

These days, there are multiple ways for you to interact with a computer system and manage it from the GUI (graphical user interface) to the CLI (command-line interface). Some people consider the latter as a huge backward step, back to the time of those old-fashioned green-screened terminals. However, today we still use it, together with web-based interfaces and API (application programming interface) calls.

But why have we gone back to the command line? To understand that, you need to understand what goes into large-scale computer system administration. Repetitive tasks take up a lot of admin time, and it is necessary to do these as quickly and efficiently as possible, especially with multiple systems requiring management. Add to that the need to make sure those tasks are done the same way every time to ensure the right results and you start to understand why the command-line interface method is so important. One of the most common command-line interfaces is Microsoft PowerShell.

What is it?

PowerShell is an automation and scripting platform developed by Microsoft. Built on the .NET framework, it combines an interactive command environment with a scripting language, and has been described by Ed Wilson, a leading resource on PowerShell, as follows:

"Windows PowerShell is an interactive object-oriented command environment with scripting language features that utilizes small programs called cmdlets to simplify configuration, administration, and management of heterogeneous environments in both standalone and networked typologies by utilizing standards-based remoting protocols."

That's quite the definition! Let's delve into it a bit deeper.

Explain Object-Oriented

In essence, an object-oriented programming language is a kind of logic, a way of understanding how a language or platform behaves. Everything in the language is an object. Python is perhaps the most famous of all object-oriented programming languages.

An object has at least one attribute and at least one method or function – have a look at some real-world examples:

- **A TV remote control** – attributes include color, shape, size, how many buttons it has, etc. Functions or methods include volume adjustment, changing channels and turning the TV on and off.
- **A vehicle** – attributes include current speed, location, license plate, etc., while methods include moving, acceleration, slowing and parking.

- **A dog** – attributes include breed, color, energy levels and mood, while methods include barking, sleeping, running, playing, etc.

Explain Cmdlets

Short for command-lets, a cmdlet is a PowerShell command and there are lots of them. Each cmdlet is responsible for a specific task or function, and we'll be covering them in detail in the next chapter. Behind a cmdlet, a lot is going on. When it is executed, the command works with multiple objects, methods, classes, API calls, and lots of other things, all to get its job done. The primary advantage of using PowerShell is that there is no need to understand all of this; the cmdlet takes care of everything.

To help you in using these cmdlets, PowerShell uses a naming pattern, verb-noun, to help you understand what each one is for. Some of the verbs you will encounter include Set, New, Get,

Copy, and Add. Putting the verbs and nouns together gives you cmdlets like:

- Get-Process
- Get-Help
- Get-Member

What Are PowerShell's Uses?

PowerShell has multiple uses and the only limit is your own creativity. The fact that its functions include scripting tools and an interactive language means that it makes system administration easy and provides IT professionals with a ton of flexibility.

When you use PowerShell as a CLI for direct system integration, you benefit from being able to connect to another system remotely. Using a remote PowerShell session, you can easily connect to a server that is in a different physical location and run commands as though you were on that server. There are lots of system tasks that can be remotely done, potentially saving you tons of time. Not only that, administrators can run the same command simultaneously on multiple servers, saving even more time.

With the PowerShell scripts, which you will also learn more about later, you can repeatedly perform repetitive tasks. One of PowerShell's biggest benefits is its ability to help you automate tasks, from rolling out new servers in virtual environments to configuring new Microsoft 365 mailboxes and everything that comes in between.

At their simplest, PowerShell scripts are nothing more than a series of commands, making it easy to transition from individual commands in a CLI to automated scripts.

What Can You Do with PowerShell?

Now you know what PowerShell is, let's look at what you can do with it.

First, keep it in mind that PowerShell is not one of those technologies that will disappear as fast as it appeared – it's here to stay. Although we moved on from CLIs and green screens, adopting GUIs for just about everything, we are going back to the old CLI methods and there are good reasons, the primary one regarding development lifecycles.

A GUI is typically a wrapper that runs commands or codes on the backend when something happens – a mouse click, for example. The code underlying it has to be written so the GUI can do its job. By eliminating the graphical part and using the code written in PowerShell, it is much faster to roll out updates and changes without the need to worry about updating a GUI and testing it, along with the code, which takes a lot of time.

Virtually all of Microsoft's products come with PowerShell integrated; indeed, some actions cannot be done with a GUI, only with PowerShell, including some actions in Server 2016 and Microsoft 365. And not only is PowerShell vital for some tasks, being able to use automation makes it worth any IT professional learning and understanding it.

When you fully understand what PowerShell is capable of, it opens up a lot of doors. From automating basic, repetitive tasks to writing advanced scripts, PowerShell offers plenty of functions and timesaving abilities.

In the next few chapters, we will take a deeper dive into PowerShell and what you can do with it, starting with an in-depth look at PowerShell cmdlets.

Chapter 2: PowerShell Cmdlets

Developers love PowerShell because of the functionality, power, and flexibility it gives the Windows Command prompt. However, although it is relatively simple to learn, there is still a learning curve to it.

PowerShell runs on commands, known as cmdlets. These are what drive its functional capabilities and give it the power it has to make your life easier. This chapter will go over some of the most important cmdlets for anyone just getting started in PowerShell.

Basic PowerShell Cmdlets

These are the basic cmdlets that help you gain information, draw up basic reports, and configure security.

1. **Get-Command**

This is one of the easiest reference cmdlets to use, giving you a list of all the commands you can use in the current session. To use it, type this command:

Get-Command

You will see something that looks a bit like this:

CommandType	Name	Definition
-----------	----	----------
Cmdlet	Add-Content	[-Path] <String[...
Cmdlet	Add-History	[[-InputObject] ...
Cmdlet	Add-Member	[-MemberType]

2. **Get-Help**

This is an essential command for any PowerShell user, and it gives you easy access to help about the commands available to you in your current session. For example, you could type the following command:

Get-Help [[-Name] <String>] [-Path <String>] [-Category <String[]>] [-Component <String[]>]

[-Functionality <String[]>] [-Role <String[]>] [-Examples] [<CommonParameters>]

3. **Set-ExecutionPolicy**

By default, scripting is disabled by Microsoft to stop malicious scripts from being executed in PowerShell. Obviously, developers need to be able to write scripts and execute them, so this command allows them to control the security that surrounds PowerShell scripts. There are four security levels available:

- **Restricted** – the default level that stops scripts from being able to run and only allows commands to be entered interactively.

- **All Signed** – this level enables scripts to run ONLY if a trustworthy publisher has signed them.

- **Remote Signed** – this level enables locally created scripts to run. Remotely created scripts can run ONLY if a reputable publisher has signed them.

- **Unrestricted** – this level removes the restrictions from the policy and enables all scripts to run.

If you are not familiar with the environment you are working in, you can use the following command to see what the current execution policy is:

Get-ExecutionPolicy

4. **Get-Service**

If you want to know the installed services on your system, you can get that information by using this command:

Get-Service

You should see something like this on your screen:

Status Name DisplayName

------ ---- -----------

Running AdobeActiveFile... Adobe Active File Monitor V4

Stopped Alerter

Running ALG Application Layer Gateway Service

Stopped AppMgmt Application Management

Running ASChannel Local Communication Channel

If you are looking for a specific service, add the -Name switch and the service name; Windows will display the service state. You can also use the built-in filtering abilities to return a subset of those services installed. If you were to use the following example, you would see the data from the Get-Service command that was piped to the cmdlet called Where-Object; this will then filter out all services other than those that have stopped:

Get-Service | Where-Object {$_.status -eq "stopped"}

5. ConvertTo-HTML

This one is pretty self-explanatory; it allows you to extract data for use in reports or send it on to someone else. Using it requires that the output from another command be piped to ConvertTo-HTML and the -Property switch to be used for specifying the output properties to go in the HTML file. A file name is also required.

As an example, the code below will result in an HTML page being created and listing the current console's PowerShell aliases:

PS C:\> get-alias | convertto-html > aliases.htm

PS C:\> invoke-item aliases.htm

You can also use the Export-CSV cmdlet to export the data into a .CSV file. To do this, specify the required properties by using the Select-Object command.

6. Get-EventLog

PowerShell makes it easy to parse the event logs on your machine with the Get-EventLog cmdlet. This one has a few parameters you can use, for example, if you wanted to see a specific log, you would use the -Log switch with the log file name. The following command will let you see the Application log:

Get-EventLog -Log "Application"

Some of the other parameters you can use are:

- -Verbose
- -Debug
- -ErrorAction
- -ErrorVariable

- -WarningAction
- -WarningVariable
- -OutBuffer
- -OutVariable

7. **Get-Process**

Sometimes, in the same way that you can get a list of all the available services, you can also get a list of the processes currently running on your system using the Get-Process command.

If you have processes that are not responding or have frozen, the Stop-Process command will let you stop them. If you know that something is holding you up but are not sure what, use Get-Process to identify it and then Stop-Process to stop it.

For example, if you wanted to stop Notepad running on your system, you would use the following command:

Stop-Process -processname notepad

Wildcard characters can also be used. In the following example, all Notepad instances will be terminated along with any process that starts with note:

Stop-Process -processname note*

8. Clear-History

If you want to clear your command history of all entries, this is the cmdlet to do it. This command can be used for deleting specific commands too. For example, if you wanted to delete all commands that contained 'help' or ended in 'command' you would use the following command:

PS C:\> Clear-History -Command *help*, *command

You can also add entries to your current session using the Add-History cmdlet.

9. Where-Object

This is one of the most important of all the PowerShell cmdlets, allowing you to pass a dataset down the pipeline to be filtered:

Get-Service | Where-Object {$_.Status -eq 'Running'}

The output should look something like this:

Status Name DisplayName

------ ---- -----------

Running AdobeARMservice Adobe Acrobat Update Service

Running AppHostSvc Application Host Helper Service

Running Appinfo Application Information

Running AudioEndpointBu... Windows Audio Endpoint Builder

Running Audiosrv Windows Audio

Running BFE Base Filtering Engine

Running BITS Background Intelligent Transfer Ser...

Running BrokerInfrastru... Background Tasks Infrastructure Ser...

Running Browser Computer Browser

Running CDPSvc Connected Devices Platform Service

10. **Set-AuthenticodeSignature**

This cmdlet allows you to keep any work in production secure and disable it from being modified by adding an Authenticode signature to your file or script:

> Set-AuthenticodeSignature somescript.ps1 @(Get-ChildItem cert:\CurrentUser\My -codesigning)[0] -IncludeChain "All" - TimestampServer

PowerShell Cmdlets to Get Things Done

PowerShell is great for productivity, providing you with these commands to let you get things done:

1. **ForEach-Object**

This cmdlet will perform an operation against each object in a specific group containing input objects. Many cmdlets will work with all objects contained in a collection, but the ForEach-Object cmdlet is required for when you want to apply specific formatting to every object or make some other modification. As an example, you can use the following commands to display process names rendered in cyan:

Get-Process | Write-Host $_.name -foregroundcolor cyan

However, that would throw up this error message:

At line:1 char:25

+ get-process | write-host <<<< $_.name -foregroundcolor cyan
Write-Host : The input object cannot be bound to any parameters for the command either because the command does not take pipeline input or the input and its properties do not match any of the parameters that take pipeline input.

Why? Because the Write-Host cmdlet doesn't know what you want to do with the data sent via the pipeline. So, the ForEach-object cmdlet is used to solve this:

Get-Process | ForEach-Object {Write-Host $_.name -foregroundcolor cyan}

2. Clear-Content

This cmdlet allows you to delete an item's content without deleting the item:

Clear-Content C:\Temp\TestFile.txt

The same command lets you clear the contents from any files with a specific extension. For example, if you wanted to remove the contents of any file with a .txt extension, you would use the following code:

Clear-Content -path * -filter *.TXT –force

3. Checkpoint-Computer

Suppose you were running a risky kind of experiment or needed to make some significant changes. You would use this cmdlet to set a restore point. However, you can only do this once in any 24-hour period with this command:

PS C:\> Checkpoint-Computer -Description "My 2nd checkpoint" -RestorePointType "Modify_Settings"

PS C:\> Get-ComputerRestorePoint | format-list

__GENUS : 2

__CLASS : SystemRestore

__SUPERCLASS :

__DYNASTY : SystemRestore

__RELPATH : SystemRestore.SequenceNumber=59

__PROPERTY_COUNT : 5

__DERIVATION : {}

__SERVER : CLIENT2

__NAMESPACE : root\default

__PATH   :
\\CLIENT2\root\default:SystemRestore.SequenceNumber=59

CreationTime : 20120202180537.316029-000

Description : My 2nd checkpoint

EventType : 100

RestorePointType : 12

SequenceNumber : 59

4. **Compare-Object**

Sometimes, you want to be able to directly compare two objects, and this cmdlet will let you do that and will also provide a report on the differences between them:

PS G:\lee\tools> cd c:\temp

PS C:\temp> $set1 = "A","B","C"

PS C:\temp> $set2 = "C","D","E"

PS C:\temp> Compare-Object $set1 $set2

InputObject SideIndicator

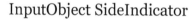

D =>

E =>

A <=

B <=

5. **ConvertFrom-StringData**

This cmdlet will let you convert a string that has at least one value pair into a hash table. As an example, you could use this command:

$settings = $TextData | ConvertFrom-StringData

You can use this cmdlet in many situations, such as when you want to save a script's settings so that others can edit them without having to go directly into the script code.

6. ConvertTo-SecureString

This cmdlet will let you convert a standard string that has been encrypted, or some plain text, into secure strings. You can use this together with Read-Host and ConvertFrom-SecureString:

ConvertTo-SecureString [-String] SomeString

ConvertTo-SecureString [-String] SomeString [-SecureKey SecureString] ConvertTo-SecureString [-String] SomeString [-Key Byte[]] ConvertTo-SecureString [-String] SomeString [-AsPlainText] [-Force]

7. ConvertTo-XML

You can use this cmdlet to create XML-based object representations, a process known as serialization and useful for when you want to save data for reuse later on. Be aware that your expression must write the objects to the pipeline; if you use Write-Host, you can't write to the pipeline and thus those objects cannot be serialized. Here's an example of the code in use:

Get-Service wuauserv -ComputerName chi-dc04,chi-p50,chi-core01 |

Export-Clixml -Path c:\work\wu.xml

In this example, we used the **Export-Clixml** cmdlet, which is ideal for lots of purposes. That cmdlet will convert an expression's output into XML and place it into a file.

8. **New-AppLockerPolicy**

You can use the New-AppLockerPolicy cmdlet to create new Applocker policies from rule creation options such as file information lists. There are five separate cmdlets that allow interaction with Applocker:

Get-AppLockerFileInformation: Gets the required information for creating AppLocker rules from a list of files or the event log.

Get-AppLockerPolicy: Used to retrieve a local, effective, or a domain AppLocker policy.

New-AppLockerPolicy: As mentioned, this cmdlet is used for creating new AppLocker policies.

Set-AppLockerPolicy: Sets the AppLocker policy for a specified group policy object.

Test-AppLockerPolicy: Used to determine if a user or group of users will be able to perform certain actions based on the policy.

9. New-ItemProperty

This cmdlet allows you to create new properties for items and set their values. It is used for creating registry values and data, for example registry key properties, and changing them.

10. New-Object

You can use this cmdlet to create instances of COM (Component Object Model) or .NET Framework objects. The following example shows you how to use it for creating a new object, storing it in a variable, and then piping it to the **Add-Member** command. This will then add the specified methods or properties:

$ourObject = New-Object -TypeName psobject

$ourObject | Add-Member -MemberType NoteProperty -Name ComputerName -Value $computerInfo.Name

$ourObject | Add-Member -MemberType NoteProperty -Name OS -Value $osInfo.Caption

```
$ourObject | Add-Member -MemberType NoteProperty -Name
'OS   Version'   -Value   $("$($osInfo.Version)   Build
$($osInfo.BuildNumber)")
```

```
$ourObject | Add-Member -MemberType NoteProperty -Name
Domain -Value $computerInfo.Domain
```

```
$ourObject | Add-Member -MemberType NoteProperty -Name
Workgroup -Value $computerInfo.Workgroup
```

```
$ourObject | Add-Member -MemberType NoteProperty -Name
DomainJoined -Value $computerInfo.Workgroup
```

```
$ourObject | Add-Member -MemberType NoteProperty -Name
Disks -Value $diskInfo
```

```
$ourObject | Add-Member -MemberType NoteProperty -Name
AdminPasswordStatus -Value $adminPasswordStatus
```

```
$ourObject | Add-Member -MemberType NoteProperty -Name
ThermalState -Value $thermalState
```

11. New-WebServiceProxy

This is another useful cmdlet for creating web service proxy objects for using the web service within PowerShell. It's a really useful cmdlet for developers as it negates the need for loads of complicated code – all they have to do is call on an already existing service to do the same job. Have a look at an example:

```
$url = http://<webapp>.azurewebsites.net/CreateSite.asmx
```

```
$proxy = New-WebServiceProxy $url
```

```
$spAccount = "<username>"
```

```
$spPassword = Read-Host -Prompt "Enter password" –
AsSecureString
```

```
$projectGuid = ""
```

```
$createOneNote = $false
```

And the following code shows you a list of all the methods available:

```
$proxy | gm -memberType Method
```


12. New-WSManInstance

This works in much the same way as the New-WebServiceProxy in that it lets you create new management resource instances:

New-WSManInstance winrm/config/Listener

-SelectorSet @{Address="*";Transport="HTTPS"}

-ValueSet
@{Hostname="Test01";CertificateThumbprint="01F7EB07A45
31750D920CE6A588BF5"}

13. **New-WsManSessionOption**

This cmdlet allows you the creation of new management session hash tables. These are then used as input parameters to a few other cmdlets for WS-Management, including:

Get-WSManInstance

Set-WSManInstance

Invoke-WSManAction

Connect-WSMan

The syntax for this cmdlet is:

New-WSManSessionOption [-NoEncryption] [-
OperationTimeout] [-ProxyAccessType] [-ProxyAuthentication]
[-ProxyCredential] [-SkipCACheck] [-SkipCNCheck] [-
SkipRevocationCheck] [-SPNPort] [-UseUTF16]
[<CommonParameters>]

14. **Select-Object**

This cmdlet lets you choose specific properties of one or a group of objects. It can also help you choose unique objects from arrays or specific objects from the start or the end of the array:

PS > Get-Process | Sort-Object name -Descending | Select-Object -Index 0,1,2,3,4

Other cmdlets that work in much the same way are:

Select-String: Finds text in strings or files.

Select-XML: Finds text in an XML string or document.

15. **Set-Alias**

This is one of the best productivity-enhancing cmdlets, allowing you to set aliases for specific command elements or cmdlets in a current session. This is much like a keyboard shortcut and enables faster working. In this example, we are setting Notepad to an alias of np:

New-Alias np c:\windows\system32\notepad.exe

16. **Set-StrictMode**

This cmdlet is used for establishing coding rules and enforcing them in expressions, script blocks and scripts. It's a great cmdlet to enforce the quality of your code and stops you writing bad code when you are tired. There are two parameters that can be used - -Version and -Off. The former, -Version has three potential values:

Version 1.0 stops you from using any variable that you haven't initialized

Version 2.0 stops you using uninitialized variables and stops you from calling a function such as a method, non-existent object properties, and stops you from creating unnamed variables

Version Latest chooses the latest version of StrictMode to use, a good option because the latest version is always used no matter what PowerShell version you are running

17. **Wait-Job**

This cmdlet stops the command prompt until there are no more background jobs running. It will not show you any output from the jobs, but you can use it with Receive-Job. And thanks to -Jobs, you can also use multithreading in PowerShell:

```
### Start-MultiThread.ps1 ###

$Computers = @("Computer1","Computer2","Computer3")


#Start all jobs
```

```powershell
ForEach($Computer in $Computers){

Start-Job     -FilePath     c:ScriptGet-OperatingSystem.ps1     -
ArgumentList $Computer

}


#Wait for all jobs

Get-Job | Wait-Job


#Get all job results

Get-Job | Receive-Job | Out-GridView


### Start-MultiThread.ps1 ###

$Computers = @("Computer1","Computer2","Computer3")


#Start all jobs

ForEach($Computer in $Computers){

Start-Job     -FilePath     c:ScriptGet-OperatingSystem.ps1     -
ArgumentList $Computer

}
```

```
#Wait for all jobs

Get-Job | Wait-Job


#Get all job results

Get-Job | Receive-Job | Out-GridView
```

18. **Write-Progress**

Everyone loves status bars and this cmdlet shows you one in the command window, allowing you to monitor what you are doing. The example below shows how to get a full bar and the runtime strings:

```
$TotalSteps = 4

$Step = 1

$StepText = "Setting Initial Variables"

$StatusText = '"Step
$($Step.ToString().PadLeft($TotalSteps.Count.ToString().Leng
th)) of $TotalSteps | $StepText"'

$StatusBlock = [ScriptBlock]::Create($StatusText)

$Task = "Creating Progress Bar Script Block for Groups"
```

Write-Progress -Id $Id -Activity $Activity -Status (& $StatusBlock) -CurrentOperation $Task -PercentComplete ($Step / $TotalSteps * 100)

PowerShell Cmdlets for Monitoring Performance, Testing and Debugging

To finish off, we have some cmdlets that developers will find useful for troubleshooting their scripts, testing them and debugging.

1. **Debug-Process**

All developers like to debug. This cmdlet allows you to easily debug your scripts. Plus, you can use Debug-Job to debug a job, and you can use a cmdlet called Wait-Debugger, or you can set breakpoints:

PS C:\> $job = Start-Job -ScriptBlock { Set-PSBreakpoint C:\DebugDemos\MyJobDemo1.ps1 -Line 8; C:\DebugDemos\MyJobDemo1.ps1 }

PS C:\> $job

PS C:\> Debug-Job $job

2. Disable-PSBreakpoint

This cmdlet allows you to eliminate previously set breakpoints in the current console. The syntax is:

Disable-PSBreakpoint [-Breakpoint] [-PassThru] [-Confirm] [-WhatIf] []

Disable-PSBreakpoint [-Id] [-PassThru] [-Confirm] [-WhatIf] []

You can also enable breakpoints by using the Enable-PSBreakpoint cmdlet.

3. Get-Counter

This cmdlet will use real-time counter data from the Windows OS performance monitoring system and can obtain the data from remote or local computers at specified sample intervals. The example below shows you how to set a counter with a maximum specified sample:

PS C:\> Get-Counter -Counter "\Processor(_Total)\% Processor Time" -SampleInterval 2 -MaxSamples 3

And the code below lets you get data from more than one computer:

The first command saves the **Disk Reads/sec** counter path in the $DiskReads variable.

PS C:\> $DiskReads = "\LogicalDisk(C:)\Disk Reads/sec"

The next command is using the pipeline operator (|) to pass the $DiskReads variable counter path to the cmdlet called **Get-Counter**. The output is limited to 10 samples using the **MaxSamples** parameter.

PS C:\> $DiskReads | Get-Counter -Computer Server01, Server02 -MaxSamples 10

4. **Export-Counter**

This one is used for exporting PerformanceCounterSampleSet objects. They are exported as counter log files and there are two available properties:

CounterSamples: Gets and sets the counter data.

Timestamp: Gets and sets date and time of the sample data.

There are also multiple methods available for inheritance from Object:

Equals(Object)

Finalize()

GetHashCode()

GetType()

MemberwiseClone()

ToString()

The command below, for example, collects the Processor Time data using Export-Counter and puts it in a .blg file:

Get-Counter "\Processor(*)\% Processor Time" | Export-Counter -Path C:\Temp\PerfData.blg

5. **Test-Path**

This cmdlet allows you to check a specified path to see if specific items are there. For example, if you wanted to use a particular command on a file, you might want to make sure the file actually exists, so you don't get an error message:

Test-Path C:\Scripts\Archive

There are two possible results – True if the folder is there, False, if it isn't.

6. **Get-WinEvent**

Get-WinEvent lets you see event logs in Windows. If you want to see all the available logs, use the following command:

Get-WinEvent -ListLog *

If you then wanted to look deeper at one log in particular, you can replace the * sign with the log name. To see all details, you would then pipe the output of this to Format-List:

```
Get-WinEvent -ListLog $logname | fl *
```

And to see all events in a specified log, use:

```
Get-WinEvent -LogName System
```

7. Invoke-TroubleshootingPack

PowerShell contains a series of assemblies and scripts collected together in troubleshooting packs. These help to you to troubleshoot system problems, diagnose them and repair them. To see all the packs, use the code below:

```
C:\Windows\Diagnostics\System
```

The code below can be run to see all the packs on the current system:

```
Get-ChildItem C:\Windows\Diagnostic\System
```

Then, using an elevated window, use the command below to run a troubleshooting pack:

```
Invoke-TroubleshootingPack (Get-TroubleshootingPack
C:\Windows\diagnostics\system\networking)
```

8. **Measure-Command**

You can also time PowerShell operations using the Measure-Command cmdlet. It lets you measure the length of time a script or script block runs, and you can see an example below:

Measure-Command { Mount-SPContentDatabase −Name wss_content_portal −WebApplication http://portal.contoso.com }

You will get a TimeSpan object as the output, containing several properties like Second, Minute, Hour, etc. and the output can be tailored to how you want it.

9. **Measure-Object**

If you want to know the size of a specific object, use the Measure-Object cmdlet. This will tell you all the numeric properties of the object, including lines, words and characters in string objects, for example, a text file.

All you have to do is provide the name and what measurement type you want performed. There are also parameters to include:

-Sum: adds values

-Average: calculates the average value

-Minimum: finds the minimum value

-Maximum: finds the maximum value

As an example, the following command sums the property values for VirtualMemorySize for the process objects:

Get-Process | measure VirtualMemorySize -Sum

10. New-Event

As you may have guessed, this cmdlet lets you create new events. You can also use New-EventLog to create event logs and event sources on remote or local computers. If you have a PowerShell-supported automation engine, it makes sense to set event logs up that log every PowerShell message. The following example shows you how Custom Logging is implemented in Event Viewer:

First, create the event log, LogName:

New-EventLog -LogName Troubleshooting_Log -Source FalloutApp

Then, to have messages sent to it, the following should be run with the cmdlet called Write-Log:

Write-EventLog -log Troubleshooting_Log -source FalloutApp - EntryType Information -eventID 10 -Message "FalloutApp has been successfully installed"

11. **Receive-Job**

If you want to know the results of any background jobs in your current session, this cmdlet will help you get them. Typically, you use this after starting a job using Start-Job and you want the results of that job:

Receive-Job -Name HighMemProcess

12. **Register-EngineEvent**

You can use this cmdlet to subscribe to any events the PowerShell engine generates with the New-Event cmdlet. As an example, you can use the command below to subscribe when the current session has exited, and the information will be saved to a log file:

Register-EngineEvent PowerShell.Exiting

-Action {"PowerShell exited at " + (Get-Date) | Out-File c:\log.txt -Append}

13. **Register-ObjectEvent**

This is much like the Register-EngineEvent cmdlet but, this time, you are subscribing to .Net Framework Object events. Have a look at the following example:

```
Register-ObjectEvent -InputObject $MyObject -EventName
OnTransferProgress -SourceIdentifier Scp.OnTransferProgress `
```

```
-Action {$Global:MCDPtotalBytes = $args[3];
$Global:MCDPtransferredBytes = $args[2]}
```

```
Register-ObjectEvent -InputObject $MyObject -EventName
OnTransferEnd `
```

```
-SourceIdentifier        Scp.OnTransferEnd        -Action
{$Global:MCDPGetDone = $True}
```

A couple more Register cmdlets that could be useful are:

Register-PSSessionConfiguration: this create a session configuration and registers it.

Register-WmiEvent: This subscribes to specified WMI events.

14. **Remove-Event**

You would use this cmdlet when you want an event removed. If you want an event log removed, you would need to use the Remove-EventLog cmdlet – this deletes the log, or alternatively, you can use it to unregister an event source. Also, you can cancel a subscription to an event using Unregister-Event without deleting the event from the queue.

15. Set-PSDebug

You would use this cmdlet to enable or disable the debugging features, set the trace levels, and turn StrictMode on or off. When you use this cmdlet at the start of your script, following the param() statement if you used one. It will eliminate errors on scripts where there is little troubleshooting information supplied by PowerShell. Have a look at this example:

```
Set-PSDebug -Strict
```

```
$Succeeded = test-path
C:\ProjectX\Src\BuiltComponents\Release\app.exe
```

```
if ($Succeeded) {

"yeah"

}

else {

"doh"
```

```
}
```

PS C:\Temp> .\foo.ps1

The variable $Succeeded cannot be retrieved because it has not been set yet.

At C:\Temp\foo.ps1:6 char:14

+ if ($Succeeded) <<<< {

16. **Start-Sleep**

If you want activity in a session or script suspended, this is the cmdlet to use. It will stop the activity for the length of time you specify:

Start-Sleep -Seconds xxx

Start-Sleep -Milliseconds xxx

If, on the other hand, you wanted running services paused, you would need to use the Suspend-Service cmdlet.

17. **Tee-Object**

The Tee-Object cmdlet is ideal for seeing command outputs when you want to analyze the quality or performance of your code. The cmdlet will store the output in a separate variable or file and, if it is the last one in a pipeline, it will display it on the console. If it isn't, it gets sent down the pipeline. The syntax is:

Tee-Object [-FilePath] <string> [-InputObject <psobject>] [<CommonParameters>]

Tee-Object -Variable <string> [-InputObject <psobject>] [<CommonParameters>]

18. **Test-AppLockerPolicy**

This cmdlet will help you evaluate if a specified input file is allowed to run for a user. The decision is based on the AppLocker policy for the file and/or user:

Test-AppLockerPolicy [-PolicyObject] -Path [-User] [-Filter >] []

Test-AppLockerPolicy [-XMLPolicy] -Path [-User] [-Filter] [<parameters>]

19. **Test-ComputerSecureChannel**

You can test connections between local computers and their domains and repair them if needed using this cmdlet. Before we had this command, the computer would need to be removed from the domain and then reconnected to try to establish a relationship. This cmdlet can save IT professionals a good deal of time. Local administrators can run this command:

Test-ComputerSecureChannel –credential
WINDOWSITPRO\Administrator –Repair

20.**Test-Path**

This cmdlet will help you see if all path elements exist, i.e. handling any errors before they can happen. The result is one of two outputs – True or False:

PS C:\> test-path c:\

True

PS C:\> test-path z:\foo

False

21. **Trace-Command**

This cmdlet is used for configuring and starting traces of given expressions or commands. You will also need Get-TraceSource to find specific names with the use of wildcards:

PS> Get-TraceSource -Name *param*

The output can be filtered depending on the pattern you want and, once a potential trace name has been identified, Trace-Command will tell you what you want to know. Have a look at the example below:

[CmdletBinding(DefaultParameterSetName = 'Host')]

param (

ScriptBlock that will be traced.

[Parameter(

ValueFromPipeline = $true,

Mandatory = $true,

HelpMessage = 'Expression to be traced'

)]

[ScriptBlock]$Expression,

```
# Name of the Trace Source(s) to be traced.

[Parameter(

Mandatory = $true,

HelpMessage = 'Name of trace, see Get-TraceSource for valid
values'

)]

[ValidateScript({

Get-TraceSource -Name $_ -ErrorAction Stop

})]

[string[]]$Name,


# Option to leave only trace information

# without actual expression results.

[switch]$Quiet,


# Path to file. If specified - trace will be sent to file instead of
host.

[Parameter(ParameterSetName = 'File')]

[ValidateScript({
```

```powershell
Test-Path $_ -IsValid
})]
[string]$FilePath
)


begin {
if ($FilePath) {
# assume we want to overwrite trace file
$PSBoundParameters.Force = $true
} else {
$PSBoundParameters.PSHost = $true
}
if ($Quiet) {
$Out = Get-Command Out-Null
$PSBoundParameters.Remove('Quiet') | Out-Null
} else {
$Out = Get-Command Out-Default
}
```

```
}


process {

Trace-Command @PSBoundParameters | &amp; $Out

}

}
```

PS> New-Alias -Name tre -Value Trace-Expression

PS> Export-ModuleMember -Function * -Alias *

22. **Write-Debug**

Our last useful cmdlet lets you write debug messages to your console. By default, adding this to a script or function will not do anything. It is waiting until $DebugPreference is modified or the -debug switch is activated when a script or function is called. If you set $DebugPreference to 'inquire' if you activate the switch, a breakpoint is created, allowing you to get into debug mode easily. Here's an example:

function Get-FilewithDebug

```
{
```

```
[cmdletbinding()]

Param

(

[parameter(Mandatory)]

[string]$path

)

Write-Verbose "Starting script"

Write-Debug "`$path is: $path"

$return = Get-ChildItem -Path $path -Filter *.exe -Recurse -Force

Write-Debug "`$return has $($return.count) items"

$return

}
```

When you run that with -debug, you get the following:

```
[C:\git] > Get-FilewithDebug -path C:\Users\jmorg_000\ -Debug

DEBUG: $path is: C:\Users\jmorg_000\
```

Confirm

Continue with this operation?

[Y] Yes [A] Yes to All [H] Halt Command [S] Suspend [?] Help
(default is "Y")

While there are many more cmdlets, these are the most common
and most useful ones. In the next chapter, we look at how to use
these to put a script together.

Chapter 3: PowerShell Scripts

Before we look into scripts, let's get a bit more background on the PowerShell language. It was developed by Microsoft as a high-level programming syntax with the purpose of allowing system admins the opportunity to automate their configurations and actions. While it is based on the standards for object-oriented languages, it is only for use in Windows, is underpinned by C# code and belongs to the .NET framework. That said, you don't need to know C# to understand PowerShell.

Perhaps the best comparison in terms of languages is Perl, commonly used for much the same functions in Linux. The PowerShell language is made up of functions known as cmdlets, each of which has at least one defined action and can return .NET objects.

What is the PowerShell ISE?

When you write a PowerShell cmdlet, you can do it in any word processing program or text editor, but in the latest Windows 10 versions you will find the PowerShell Integrated Scripting Environment (ISE), which is designed to make it easier to script.

When you first open the ISE, it will look much like a command-line interface with a prompt. However, it is packed with support and functionality to help you write your scripts. You will find a list of common cmdlets and modules is easily accessible and, when you begin writing scripts, a handy debugging tool lets you test your scripts, find any problems, and repair them.

Like most coding environments, the ISE can be customized to your requirements – you can change the color, theme, font, and much more. When you create a new script, the ISE will save it with the .psi extension, indicating it can only run in a PowerShell environment. If you are familiar with the Windows command prompt, the PowerShell scripting language will be easier to use, with data piping, objects, ping, and more, working in much the same way. However, the main difference is that the PowerShell syntax is much easier to read and understand than Windows command prompt commands.

Features and Uses of PowerShell

Windows PowerShell has many uses, but the primary benefit for the beginner is that scripts can be used for system automation, in terms of:

- Working with large file batches, to automate system backups or have access control over multiple files at the same time.
- PowerShell Scripts also help administrators to add users and remove them. With one carefully written script, the

processes of updating the security software, adding a network drive and giving new users permission to access specific files can easily be automated.

All of this requires that you use multiple PowerShell features, including aliases and cmdlets, which we'll talk about shortly.

How to Launch PowerShell

The easiest way to launch PowerShell is to use the search bar. Simply go to the taskbar, type in powershell and click the result. If you want to run it as an administrator, right-click on the result and then click on Run as Administrator.

Before You Run a PowerShell Script

We're going to be creating a script or two in this chapter and they will be saved as .ps1 files. You will not be able to run these by double-clicking on them, as Windows won't allow it by default. Why? Because poor or malicious scripts can do a lot of damage to a system, even accidentally. Instead, right-click the file and click on the option to Run with PowerShell.

However, if this is your first time using PowerShell, you might find this doesn't work. A system-wide policy stops scripts from executing so, to find out what it is, open the ISE and type the following at the prompt:

Get-ExecutionPolicy

You should see one of these on your screen:

- **Restricted** – scripts cannot be executed. This is default and must be changed.

- **AllSigned** – the only scripts that can run are those that a trusted developer has signed. Before you can run any script, you will get a prompt.

- **RemoteSigned** – any script can be run but you should not have this option enabled.

The policy setting must be changed before you can run any scripts, so set it to RemoteSigned. Open the command prompt and run this command:

Set-ExecutionPolicy RemoteSigned

Now you can start.

Finding PowerShell Commands

PowerShell is incredibly powerful, but behind that is a significant level of complexity. You cannot possibly remember every single command, filter, flag, alias, and more, and PowerShell doesn't expect you to. The editor contains a ton of useful tools that help you deal with this, and the following are the commonly used ones:

- **Tab Completion** – you do not need to remember every command name or how to spell them; if you type get-c at the prompt and start pressing the tab key, you will see the commands that start with the letter or letters that you started inputting. You can do this at any time during a command, not just with command names but with paths and flags too.

- **Get-Command** – tab completion is great, but it can only work if you know which command name you want. If you don't know the name, you need to use a different command: Get-Command. Be aware that commands have a VERB-NOUN syntax and typically start with SET, GET, READ, WRITE, and so on. The noun part of the syntax is things like servers, files, things from applications, and network. Get-Command will show you all the available commands on your current system.

- **Command Syntax** – the Perl language was once described as looking much like "executable line noise" - a useful tool with a syntax that is quite opaque and that has a high learning curve. The Windows command prompt, although not quite the same is very near to it. Think about this - a common job is looking in a directory for all items that start with a string of 'Foo'. In Perl, you'll see the following:

CMD: FOR /D /r %G in ("Foo*") DO @Echo %G

Breaking this down:

- **FOR and DO** – this tells us it is a loop
- **/D Flag** – this tells us that it is for Directories
- **/r Flag** – tells us that "Files Rooted at Path"
- **'in'** – designates the pattern defining the files for looping over
- **@Echo** – tells the script to write each loop's results
- **%G** – is an 'implicit parameter' – the only reason it is known as 'G' is that the a, d, f, n, o, s, t and x pathname format letters have already been used by other developers, and G provides the biggest set of "unused" letters that can be used for returned variables – G, H, I, J, K, L and M – a not too pretty hack.

Now let's look at the equivalent in PowerShell:

Get-ChildItem -Path C:\Example -Filter 'Foo*'

Much neater, yes? The output has much the same functionality, but it is so much easier to understand. Something that may not be too obvious is the wildcard - *. This was in both the examples and is telling the command to look for items beginning with 'Foo", regardless of what they end with.

And it gets better. Let's say that you wanted to identify files in the path and not directories. You could mess around with the command-line version if you like, but it is much easier to use PowerShell.

Running a PowerShell Script

You can make a script in two primary ways:

1. This is familiar to those who use the Windows Command Line – writing your scripts in Notepad. Open a new file in Notepad and write in the following:

Write-Host "Hello World!"

Save it with the name, FirstScript.ps1. That script can be called upon via PowerShell with the following command:

& "X:\FirstScript.ps1"

The output will show up in the PowerShell console.

2. This is a more powerful way – using the PowerShell ISE which lets you run and debug scripts in the GUI. The ISE also provides useful features such as multiline editing, syntax highlighting, selective execution, tab completion and many more. And you can open more than one script

window at once, which is useful considering some of your scripts may need to call on others.

You might think it's a bit much right now, but you should consider using the ISE from the start. This will give you time to get used to it before you work on complex scripts.

Examples of Basic PowerShell Scripts

Now you are ready to start writing some PowerShell scripts.

Example Script One – Get the Date

This is a nice simple script to begin with. Using Notepad or the ISE, open a file and type in the following:

Write-Host get-date

Save the file, naming it as GetDate.ps1

Use the following command to call the script through PowerShell:

& "C:\GetDate.ps1"

The output will appear in PowerShell.

Example Script Two – Force Stop A Process

A PowerShell script can be used to stop a frozen Windows service. Let's say, for example, that your company uses Lync as a business communication service. It continually freezes, causing problems, and has a process ID of 9212 – we can use a script to stop it.

As you did earlier, open a new file and type in:

stop-process 9212

or

stop-process -processname lync

Save your script and name it StopLync.ps1. Invoke it via Powershell with the following command:

& "X:\StopLync.ps1"

You can expand this script to stop multiple processes at the same time simply by adding the right commands to the file. Another script could be written to start multiple processes at the same time:

start-process -processname [your process here]

This is very useful if you want multiple networking processes started at the same time and don't want to waste time inputting several commands.

Example Script Three – Check to See If a File Exists

Let's say you want to delete several files at once; first, you should check that they exist. A command called test-patch tells you whether certain elements of a path are there. If the elements are there, TRUE is returned; if not, FALSE is returned. Just type the following:

test-Path (the file path)

Example Script Four – Set a VPN up On a New Machine

Now you understand the script basics, we can write a script to do something useful. One of the biggest advantages of PowerShell, especially for system administrators, is its ability to automate the setting up of new machines. Today, many businesses and individuals use VPNs (virtual private networks) as a way of securing their data, and any new machine added to the system should be connected to that VPN at the time they are set up. Sure, you could do this manually, but PowerShell makes the job so much easier. With PowerShell, we can write a script that sets up and configures it automatically. The easiest way to do it is to open a new file and add this command to it:

Set-VpnConnection -Name "Test1" -ServerAddress "10.1.1.2" - PassThru

Set the server address to the local VPN server address, and the -PassThru command will ensure the VPN configuration options are returned.

Save the file, name it SetVPN.ps1 and then invoke it:

```
& "X:\SetVPN.ps1"
```

PowerShell Punctuation

In summary, below is a table showing you some of the punctuation you may have seen used in this chapter:

Symbol	Name	Function	Example
$	Dollar Symbol	Used for declaring variables	$a
=	Equals Symbol	Used for assigning values to variables	$a=get-date
""	Double Quotes	Used to display text	If $a=Tuesday "Day of week: $a" will have an output of Day of week Tuesday
+	Plus Symbol	Used for concatenation	$a=October "Day of week:" + $a.Dayofweek will output October Tuesday
()	Parenthesis Symbol	Used to group arguments	(get-date).day

Chapter 4: PowerShell Strings and Quotes

One of the most used data types in any programming language, especially PowerShell, is the string type. It is used for all sorts of things, including input prompts, message displays, and even putting data in files. In fact, it's fair to say that to write a script, you need strings.

In this chapter, we will look at what strings are and what they can do. You can manipulate them for just about any purpose you want. You can use them for replacing words, characters, concatenation, splitting strings, and much more!

Understanding Strings

The .NET documentation defines a string as "a sequential collection of characters that is used to represent text". If you have a sequence of any number of characters forming a piece of text, you have a string.

Defining Strings

A string must be defined by being enclosed in single quotes or doubles as you can see in the examples below:

PS> 'Hello PowerShell - Today is $(Get-Date)'

PS> "Hello PowerShell - Today is $(Get-Date)"

The first example string has a pair of single quotes and the second has double quotes. There is only one difference between them – when you enclose a string in double quotes, it supports expansion of that string; single quotes are used for representing literal strings.

To demonstrate that, look at the screenshot below – a string enclosed in single quotes will return the exact text in the quotes; the string with double quotes will return the enclosed string and the result of the cmdlet, Get-Date:

```
PS C:\> 'Hello PowerShell - Today is $(Get-Date)'
Hello PowerShell - Today is $(Get-Date)          ←———  Single Quote Output (Literal)
PS C:\> "Hello PowerShell - Today is $(Get-Date)"
Hello PowerShell - Today is 03/24/2020 01:19:53  ←———  Double Quote Output (Expanded)
```

This shows you when you should use single or double quotes, but we will dig into this in more detail at the end of the chapter. For now, more about strings.

String Object

So, a string is a series of characters forming a text and the result from this string is called a string object, which is a .NET object of the type, [System.String]. Because a string is an object, it contains properties, and you can use the Get-Member cmdlet to access these.

PS> "Hello PowerShell - Today is $(Get-Date)" | Get-Member=

In the screenshot below, you can see the TypeName and a list showing some of the string object properties.

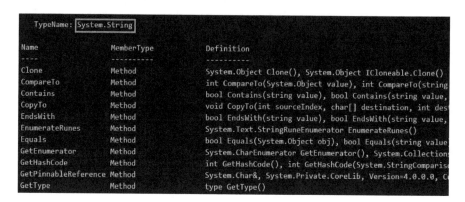

PowerShell Strings - Concatenation

Concatenation is the act of joining one string to another. You can concatenate multiple string objects to form one new string object. PowerShell has a few concatenation methods, and which one you use will depend on how you are going to implement the concatenation.

One of the best real-world examples of string concatenation is user creation in Active Directory. Let's say that you are writing a script to take the following values from a list:

- First name
- Last name
- Department

Concatenation allows you to draw up the naming conventions for the following information:

- Name
- Display name
- Username
- Email address

In the example, you will work with the following strings, so open a PowerShell session and type in the following:

$domain = 'contoso.com'

$firstname = 'Jack'

$lastname = 'Ripper'

$department = 'Health'

We want to get the following values from the variable values above:

Name = firstname lastname

DisplayName = firstname lastname (department)

SamAccountName = firstname.lastname

EmailAddress = firstname.lastname@contoso.com

Shortly, we will create those values using some of the different PowerShell methods for concatenation.

PowerShell Strings Concatenation Operator

Every programming language has a concatenation operator. Visual Basic, for example, uses the & symbol (ampersand) while PowerShell uses the + symbol (plus).

With the concatenation operator, you can use the code below to get the values you need:

Using the String Concatenation Operator

Name

$firstname + ' ' + $lastname

DisplayName

$firstname + ' ' + $lastname + ' (' + $department + ')'

SamAccountName

$firstname + '.' + $lastname

Email Address

$firstname + '.' + $lastname + '@' + $domain

The output from that should look like this:

```
PS C:\> # Using the String Concatenation Operator
PS C:\> ## Name
PS C:\> $firstname + ' ' + $lastname
Jack Ripper  ←————
PS C:\> ## DisplayName
PS C:\> $firstname + ' ' + $lastname + ' (' + $department + ')'
Jack Ripper (Health)  ←————
PS C:\> ## SamAccountName
PS C:\> $firstname + '.' + $lastname
Jack.Ripper  ←————
PS C:\> ## Email Address
PS C:\> $firstname + '.' + $lastname + '@' + $domain
Jack.Ripper@contoso.com  ←————
PS C:\> |
```

PowerShell Strings Expansion

The string expansion method is the PowerShell concatenation method that provides the shortest code. Have a look at the example below; you can see that all you need to do is put the strings in the order they should appear and use double-quotes to enclose them:

Using String Expansion

Name

"$firstname $lastname"

DisplayName

"$firstname $lastname ($department)"

SamAccountName

"$firstname.$lastname"

Email Address

"$firstname.$lastname@$domain"

PowerShell will interpret the string expansion and handle it, with the output being the concatenated string. Have a look at the example output below:

```
PS C:\> # Using String Expansion
PS C:\> ## Name
PS C:\> "$firstname $lastname"
Jack Ripper  ⬅
PS C:\> ## DisplayName
PS C:\> "$firstname $lastname ($department)"
Jack Ripper (Health) ⬅
PS C:\> ## SamAccountName
PS C:\> "$firstname.$lastname"
Jack.Ripper  ⬅
PS C:\> ## Email Address
PS C:\> "$firstname.$lastname@$domain"
Jack.Ripper@contoso.com  ⬅
PS C:\>
```

PowerShell Format Operator

The PowerShell format operator, indicated by -f, is for composite formatting, and use of the operator is in three parts. Look at the code example below; on line three you see "{0} {1}" which is used for representing the format and placeholders. The numbers are showing the index or location of the string to display.

In this example you can that $firstname, $lastname represents the string collection as the input, which means that $firstname has an index of 0 and $lastname has an index of 1. Lastly, you can see the format operator between the placeholder and string collection:

Using Format Operator

Name

"{0} {1}" -f $firstname,$lastname

DisplayName

"{0} {1} ({2})" -f $firstname,$lastname,$department

SamAccountName

"{0}.{1}" -f $firstname,$lastname

Email Address

"{0}.{1}@{2}" -f $firstname,$lastname,$domain

The output will be something similar to below.

```
PS C:\> # Using Format Operator
PS C:\> ## Name
PS C:\> "{0} {1}" -f $firstname, $lastname
Jack Ripper  ◄──────
PS C:\> ## DisplayName
PS C:\> "{0} {1} ({2})" -f $firstname,$lastname,$department
Jack Ripper (Health) ◄──────
PS C:\> ## SamAccountName
PS C:\> "{0}.{1}" -f $firstname,$lastname
Jack.Ripper  ◄──────
PS C:\> ## Email Address
PS C:\> "{0}.{1}@{2}" -f $firstname,$lastname,$domain
Jack.Ripper@contoso.com  ◄──────
PS C:\> |
```

PowerShell -Join Operator

You can use the -Join operator to join several strings into one string, and there are two ways to do this. The first is to follow the -Join operator with the string array that you want concatenated, but you do not get the option of adding a delimiter. The strings are simply joined together with nothing in between them:

-Join <String[]>

In the second method, -Join lets you specify a delimiter and the strings are joined with the delimiter in between each one:

<String[]> -Join <Delimiter>

The idea is to concatenate two or more strings, and the code below shows you how to use the operator to join them:

Using the Join Operator

Name

$firstname, $lastname -join ' '

DisplayName

$firstname,$lastname,"($department)" -join ' '

SamAccountName

-join ($firstname,'.',$lastname)

Email Address

-join ($firstname,'.',$lastname,'@',$domain)

You would see something like the output below if you ran this code:

```
PS C:\> # Using the Join Operator
PS C:\> ## Name
PS C:\> $firstname, $lastname -join ' '
Jack Ripper  ◄──────
PS C:\> ## DisplayName
PS C:\> $firstname,$lastname,"($department)" -join ' '
Jack Ripper (Health) ◄──────
PS C:\> ## SamAccountName
PS C:\> -join ($firstname,'.',$lastname)
Jack.Ripper ◄──────
PS C:\> ## Email Address
PS C:\> -join ($firstname,'.',$lastname,'@',$domain)
Jack.Ripper@contoso.com ◄──────
PS C:\> |
```

.NET String.Format() Method

This method is the .NET version of the format operator in PowerShell. It works the same way as the format operator in that you must specify the format and placeholders:

Using the Format Method

Name

[string]::Format("{0} {1}",$firstname,$lastname)

DisplayName

[string]::Format("{0} {1} ({2})",$firstname,$lastname,$department)

SamAccountName

[string]::Format("{0}.{1}",$firstname,$lastname)

Email Address

[string]::Format("{0}.{1}@{2}",$firstname,$lastname,$domain)

Below you can see how the String.Format method works:

```
PS C:\> # Using the Format Method
PS C:\> ## Name
PS C:\> [string]::Format("{0} {1}",$firstname,$lastname)
Jack Ripper  ◀────
PS C:\> ## DisplayName
PS C:\> [string]::Format("{0} {1} ({2})",$firstname,$lastname,$department)
Jack Ripper (Health) ◀────
PS C:\> ## SamAccountName
PS C:\> [string]::Format("{0}.{1}",$firstname,$lastname)
Jack.Ripper  ◀────
PS C:\> ## Email Address
PS C:\> [string]::Format("{0}.{1}@{2}",$firstname,$lastname,$domain)
Jack.Ripper@contoso.com  ◀────
PS C:\> |
```

.NET String.Concat() Method

This is the .NET version of the concatenation operator in PowerShell. However, rather than the + symbol, this one involves placing all the strings to be added inside the method, i.e. – [string]::Concat(string1,string2...).

Here's a full example:

Using the .NET String.Concat Method

Name

[string]::Concat($firstname,' ',$lastname)

DisplayName

[string]::Concat($firstname,' ',$lastname,' (',$department,')')

SamAccountName

[string]::Concat($firstname,'.',$lastname)

Email Address

[string]::Concat($firstname,'.',$lastname,'@',$domain)

In the screenshot below, you can see the result of using this method:

```
PS C:\> # Using the .NET String.Concat Method
PS C:\> ## Name
PS C:\> [string]::Concat($firstname,' ',$lastname)
Jack Ripper  ◄─────
PS C:\> ## DisplayName
PS C:\> [string]::Concat($firstname,' ',$lastname,' (',$department,')')
Jack Ripper (Health)  ◄─────
PS C:\> ## SamAccountName
PS C:\> [string]::Concat($firstname,'.',$lastname)
Jack.Ripper  ◄─────
PS C:\> ## Email Address
PS C:\> [string]::Concat($firstname,'.',$lastname,'@',$domain)
Jack.Ripper@contoso.com  ◄─────
PS C:\>
```

.NET String.Join() Method

This is the .NET version of the join operator in PowerShell and the format of the method is [string]::Join(<delimiter>,<string1>,<string2>,...).

The delimiter is ALWAYS the first item in the method, followed by the item values, which are the strings to be concatenated. The code below shows you how this works – if you don't want a delimiter, make sure you specify it this way - — >:

Using the .NET String.Join Method

Name

[string]::Join(' ',$firstname,$lastname)

DisplayName

[string]::Join(' ',$firstname,$lastname,"($department)")

SamAccountName

[string]::Join('',$firstname,'.',$lastname)

Email Address

[string]::Join('',$firstname,'.',$lastname,'@',$domain)

The result will look something like this:

```
PS C:\> # Using the .NET String.Join Method
PS C:\> ## Name
PS C:\> [string]::Join(' ',$firstname,$lastname)
Jack Ripper  ←——
PS C:\> ## DisplayName
PS C:\> [string]::Join(' ',$firstname,$lastname,"($department)")
Jack Ripper (Health) ←——
PS C:\> ## SamAccountName
PS C:\> [string]::Join('',$firstname,'.',$lastname)
Jack.Ripper ←——
PS C:\> ## Email Address
PS C:\> [string]::Join('',$firstname,'.',$lastname,'@',$domain)
Jack.Ripper@contoso.com ←——
PS C:\>
```

How to Split PowerShell Strings

Up to now we have looked at a few ways to concatenate or join strings, so now we need to look at how to split them. There are two main way to do this – with the split() method, or with the split operator.

Using the Split() Method

The simplest way to create arrays by splitting strings is by using the split() method. This is on all string objects and can split strings based on non-regex characters. Let's look at an example.

Let's say we have a string of green | eggs | and | ham and we want an array, something like @('green', 'eggs', 'and', 'ham'). The string split can be done on the pipe (|) as you can see in the code below:

$string = 'green|eggs|and|ham'

$string.split('|')

PowerShell splits the string using the pipe symbol into an output like below:

```
PS /> $string = 'green|eggs|and|ham'
PS /> $string.split('|')
green
eggs
and
ham
```

While this is a simple method of splitting strings, it is somewhat limited. It doesn't let you use regular expressions to split the strings, so, if you need to go further than this method allows, you need to understand the split operator.

The -split Operator

This is the primary method of splitting strings and it allows for the strings to be split between the default (whitespaces) or using a specified delimiter. Below, you can see the syntax for the -Split operator – take note of the difference between the unary split and the binary split:

Unary Split

-Split <String>

-Split (<String[]>)

Binary Split

<String> -Split <Delimiter>[,<Max-substrings>[,"<Options>"]]

<String> -Split {<ScriptBlock>} [,<Max-substrings>]

Here, you can see that the $string variable has a value of one single-line string. With the split operator, we can split that single line into a string array, and the split string will be saved to the variable called $split:

Splitting Strings into Substrings

Assign a string value to the $string variable

$string = 'This sentence will be split between whitespaces'

Split the value of the $string and store the result to the $split variable

$split = -split $string

Get the count of the resulting substrings

$split.Count

Show the resulting substrings

$split

Run it and you will see that one string has been split into several substrings.

Using a Character Delimiter to Split Strings

So, we looked at the split operator and how to use it for splitting one string into several, even without the use of a delimiter. The reason for this is that the default delimiter in the split operator is whitespace. However, you can also use script blocks, patterns, strings, and characters as a delimiter. In the example below, we use the semicolon (;):

Splitting Strings into Substrings with Delimiter

Assign a string value to the $string variable

```
$string = 'This;sentence;will;be;split;between;semicolons'
```

Split the value of the $string and store the result to the $split variable

```
$split = $string -split ";"
```

Get the count of the resulting substrings

```
$split.Count
```

Show the resulting substrings

```
$split
```

Run this code in PowerShell and you should see this output:

```
PS C:\> ## Splitting Strings into Substrings with Delimiter
PS C:\> # Assign a string value to the $string variable
PS C:\> $string = 'This;sentence;will;be;split;between;semicolons'
PS C:\> # Split the value of the $string and store the result to the $split variable
PS C:\> $split = $string -split ";"
PS C:\> # Get the count of the resulting substrings
PS C:\> $split.Count
7
PS C:\> # Show the resulting substrings
PS C:\> $split
This
sentence
will
be
split
between
semicolons
PS C:\>
```

You should spot that you cannot see the delimiter at all as it has been omitted from the substrings. If you want to keep the delimiter character, you can enclose it in a set of parentheses, like this:

$split = $string -split "(;)"

$split.Count

$split

Once you have modified the delimiter, run it and you should see this output:

```
PS C:\> $split = $string -split "(;)"
PS C:\> $split.Count
13 ←
PS C:\> $split
This
;
sentence
;
will
;
be
;
split
;
between
;
semicolons
PS C:\>
```

The delimiter strings are now there and are counted with the substrings.

Using a String Delimiter to Split Strings

You can also use a string to split a string; in the example below, we are using a string 'day':

$daysOfTheWeek=
'monday,tuesday,wednesday,thursday,friday,saturday,sunday'

$daysOfTheWeek -split "day"

As you would expect, the result is a split between the text, 'day'.

Using a RegEx Delimiter to Split Strings

The split operator uses Regex by default to match the delimiter specified, which means that RegEx can be used as delimiters to split the strings. In the next example, we have a string containing both word and non-word characters. We want the string split using the non-word characters and, in RegEx, \W is used to represent these while \w is used to represent the word characters that match [a-z,A-Z,0-9]:

$daysOfTheWeek=
'monday=tuesday*wednesday^thursday#friday!saturday(sund
ay'

```
$daysOfTheWeek -split "\W"
```

Run the code and the output will show you that non-word characters were used for delimiters.

Split Strings and Limit the Number of Substrings

There is also a way of stopping the split operator so that it doesn't split a string into substrings. To do that, you need to use the <Max-substrings> parameter. If you look at the syntax for the split operator, you will see that the <Max-substrings> parameter comes straight after the <Delimited> parameter. Here's the syntax again just for reference:

```
<String> -Split <Delimiter>[,<Max-substrings>[,"<Options>"]]
```

So, following that, the next code has been modified so the number of substrings is limited to 3:

```
$daysOfTheWeek=
'monday,tuesday,wednesday,thursday,friday,saturday,sunday'

$daysOfTheWeek -split ",",3
```

Running the code will show you that only three substrings are output, and the rest of the delimiters are skipped over.

Now, let's say that you wanted the substrings limited in reverse. In this case, you would use a negative value for the <Max-substrings> parameter. In our example, we change it to -3:

$daysOfTheWeek=
'monday,tuesday,wednesday,thursday,friday,saturday,sunday'

$daysOfTheWeek -split ",",-3

The result of that is that the string is split from the last three matching delimiters.

Finding and Replacing Strings

Now, we will look at two methods you can use for searching for and carrying out a string replace in PowerShell. Those two methods are the -Replace operator and the Replace() method.

The Replace() Method

We'll start with the Replace() method, which is built-in to the string object, and used for helping you in search for and replace operations. The method can take up to four overloads and the acceptable ones are shown below:

<String>.Replace(<original>, <substitute>[, <ignoreCase>][, <culture>])

Really, you only require the <substitute> and <original> overloads, while the <culture> and <ignoreCase> overloads are optional.

As you can see from the next example, the code looks for every instance of a comma character (,) with the semicolon (;):

$daysOfTheWeek   =
'monday,tuesday,wednesday,thursday,friday,saturday,sunday'

$daysOfTheWeek.Replace(',',';')

You can use the replace() method to do more than just replace one character; you can also use it for search and replace on strings too. In the code below, we are replacing one word, 'day' with another, 'night':

$daysOfTheWeek   =
'monday,tuesday,wednesday,thursday,friday,saturday,sunday'

$daysOfTheWeek.Replace('day','NIGHT')

The -Replace Operator

You can also search for and replace operations using the replace operator, and you can see the syntax for that below:

<string> -replace <original>, <substitute>

With that syntax, we are replacing 'day' with night' in the next example, using that replace operator:

```
$daysOfTheWeek                                    =
'monday,tuesday,wednesday,thursday,friday,saturday,sunday'

$daysOfTheWeek -replace 'day','NIGHT'
```

And the next code is using a RegEx match to use the replace operator for replacing the strings. We used the here-string to search on for a string matching (#.) and are replacing it with nothing:

```
$daysOfTheWeek = @'

1. Line 1

2. Line 2

3. Line 3

4. Line 4

5. Line 5

'@

$daysOfTheWeek -replace "\d.\s",""
```

Extract Strings from Strings

In the string object is another method named SubString() which is used for extracting strings from strings at specified points. Here's the syntax for SubString():

<String>.SubString(<startIndex>[,<length>])

StartIndex is placed at the position where the search by the SubString() method will start. The length parameter states how many characters are to be returned from the position of startIndex – this is an optional parameter and if you don't use it, all the characters will be returned by SubString().

Extract a Substring from a Starting Position with a Fixed Length

In the next example, we retrieve a sample of the value for the $guid string. It starts at the index of 9 and returns the 5 characters after that point:

$guid = 'e957d74d-fa16-44bc-9d72-4bea54952d8a'

$guid.SubString(9,5)

Extract a Substring from a Dynamic Starting Position

In our next example, you can use the length property to define a dynamic starting index. The code will:

- Retrieve the string object's length

- Divide the length by 2 to get the middle index's index
- Use the middle index as the start for the substring

$guid = 'e957d74d-fa16-44bc-9d72-4bea54952d8a'

$guid.SubString([int]($guid.Length/2))

Because we didn't specify the length value, all the starting index characters will be returned by the SubString() method.

How to Compare PowerShell Strings

PowerShell can also help you to compare strings and this is done with methods built into the string object; methods such as CompareTo(), Contains(), and Equals(). You can also use the comparison operators in PowerShell.

The CompareTo() Method

This method will return a 0 value if the compared strings have identical values. For example, the next code is used for comparing string objects:

$string1 = "This is a string"

$string2 = "This is a string"

$string1.CompareTo($string2)

Because they both have the same value, you should see a result of 0 when you run it.

The Equals() Method and -eq Operator

You can use both of these – the -eq operator and the Equals() method – for checking if two strings have equal values. In the next example, we use the Equals() method:

$string1 = "This is a string"

$string2 = "This is not the same string"

$string1.Equals($string2)

The output should be False because the string values do not equal one another.

The -eq Operator

Now we'll use the -eq operator to compare the values of two strings:

$string1 = "This is a string"

$string2 = "This is not the same string"

$string1 -eq $string2

From the output, you will easily see that you get the same result whether you use the Equals() method or the -eq operator.

The Contains() Method

In the next code example, we are comparing two strings by checking if one string has the substring of another. The code below shows you that the values for $string 1 and $string 2 are not the same, but that the $string2 value is a $string1 substring.

$string1 = "This is a string 1"

$string2 = "This is a string"

$string1.Contains($string2)

If you run this, you will see from the output that the result is True.

PowerShell Quotes

We briefly mentioned quotes earlier and, to finish off this chapter, we're going to take a deeper look at them.

PowerShell allows the use of two types of quote – single and double. There are important differences between them that, if you don't understand them, can make or break your scripts.

Understand the differences and your scripts will be far more effective.

'Single Quotes'

The single quotes are the ones you will use the most often and are the ones you will encounter the most when you create or troubleshoot a script in PowerShell. Have a look at this example:

Assign variable with literal value of 'single'.

$MyVar1 = 'single'

Put variable into another literal string value.

Write-Host -Message 'Fun with $MyVar1 quotes.'

Now have a look at the output:

As you can see, $MyVar1 is ignored by PowerShell; instead the variable is literally treated exactly as it was typed – as $MyVar1. It doesn't do any substitutions at all.

So, how do we get PowerShell to see the value in a string value that has been quoted? Well, that's where we need to understand the double quotes.

"Double Quotes"

Double quotes provide string values with a dynamic element and you are likely to encounter these when you have dynamic data in a string. That data comes from variables that have been generated dynamically or are stored in memory. Have a look at this example:

Same as previous example. Create variable with a simple value.

$MyVar2 = 'double'

Now a demonstration of how the double quotes work for interpretation

Write-Host -Message "Fun with $MyVar2 quotes."

Have a look at the output:

```
Administrator: C:\Program Files\PowerShell\6\pwsh.exe
PS6>$MyVar2 = 'double'
PS6>Write-Host -Message "Fun with $MyVar2 quotes."
Fun with double quotes.
PS6>
```

Double quoted string looks for $ character, and proceeds to process variable until met with a space

In this example, $MyVar 2 is processed by PowerShell because it is in a string with double quotes. This type of quote ensures that PowerShell parses for the variable that has a $ sign in front of it, and the variable name is substituted with the corresponding value.

Real World Example

Let's apply what we learned here to a real-life example. Let's say that you want a small function created to provide one of your team operators with some basic information:

Date / Time

Disk % Used

Disk % free

This information needs to be visually turned into an operator. First, we need a bit of pseudo-code. The date time must be displayed as the current date and time, so have a think about how this will work. The Get-Date cmdlet could be used with the UFormat parameter; that would have the right patterns to provide the right date and time:

$date = Get-Date -UFormat "%m / %d / %Y:"

Test this in PowerShell and you will see that it works just fine:

```
Administrator: C:\Program Files\PowerShell\6\pwsh.exe
PS6>$date = Get-Date -UFormat "%m / %d / %Y:"
PS6>$date
01 / 01 / 2019:
PS6>
```

Date format as needed.

So, that gets the first bit of the script out of the way. Now we need a bit of disk information output on the PowerShell terminal; to be more specific, we want to know how much free space remains as a percentage. We'll use Write-Host to display this, but we need a bit of extra code in our string inside double quotes.

Don't forget, this will be dynamic information so we will start by creating a variable and then get the value we want with a member type property:

$disk = Get-DiskSpace | Where-Object -Property Name -EQ 'C:\'

Again, testing this shows it works well:

```
Administrator: C:\Program Files\PowerShell\6\pwsh.exe
PS6>$disk = Get-DiskSpace | Where-Object -Property Name -EQ 'C:\'
PS6>$disk.PercentFree
15.29
PS6>
```

Pulling out an object value using a member type of the $disk variable.

Great. We now have a pair of variables that can go in the strings and the operator will see them when the function is run. So, let's put all of this together in the script that will be the function:

function Get-CurrentDiskPercentageUsed {

```
$date = Get-Date -UFormat "%m / %d / %Y:"

$disk = Get-DiskSpace | Where-Object -Property Name -EQ
'C:\'

Write-Host "Storage report for $date"

Write-Host    -ForegroundColor    Yellow    "There    is
$($disk.PercentFree)% total disk space remaining."

}
```

Run this in the terminal and something like this will appear:

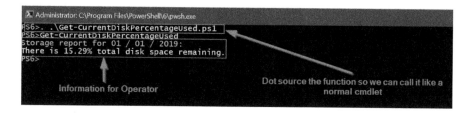

Now, did you spot what we did with the Write-Host line that has the $disk variable in it? The $() subexpression operator is evaluated by PowerShell as a whole subexpression and the result is replaced. And this will also negate the need to have to create even more variables, resulting in memory savings and a much faster script.

However, we still need to do some work to our function, so let's add a bit of math to give the operator a full calculation:

function Get-CurrentDiskPercentageUsed {

```
$date = Get-Date -UFormat "%m / %d / %Y:"

$disk = Get-DiskSpace | Where-Object -Property Name -EQ
'C:\'

    Write-Host "Storage report for $date"

    Write-Host -ForegroundColor Red "There is $(100 -
$disk.PercentFree)% total disk utilization on drive
$($disk.Name)."

    Write-Host -ForegroundColor Yellow "There is
$($disk.PercentFree)% total disk space remaining."

}
```

And the output of that is:

```
PowerShell 6 (x64)
PS6>Get-CurrentDiskPercentageUsed
Storage report for 01 / 01 / 2019:
There is 84.71% total disk utilization on drive C:\.
There is 15.29% total disk space remaining.
PS6>
```

Added some simple math to calculate percent used by subtracting from 100.

Now the operator is able to make much faster decisions while, at the same time, providing support to a remote system.

Escaping Double Quotes Using PowerShell

You now know how the single and double quotes work in PowerShell, so let's briefly discuss something a little more complex – how to escape the double quotes in a string.

You learned that variables can be expanded in strings by using the double quotes, but what happens if you need literal double quotes included in a string? In a case like that, you would need to use single quotes, or you would need to escape the double quotes.

What does 'escaping' mean? Let's take a look at an example:

We're going to create a string with double quotes, as you can see below. Note that, right now, "string" doesn't have the double quotes in it.

PS51> "string"

string

There are two ways to add the double quotes in. You could choose to use single quotes to enclose the string, or, you can use a backtick symbol to escape the double quotes. Here's an example of both options in PowerShell – note that we now have the double quotes in "string":

PS51> '"string"'

"string"

PS51> "`"string`""

"string"

There really isn't a great deal to learn with PowerShell quotes, but you do need to remember one key concept – you must know when to be dynamic and when to be literal. Use single quotes unless your string data is dynamic, it's as simple as that.

In the next chapter, we'll take a look at PowerShell automation.

Chapter 5: Automating Tasks Using PowerShell

In this chapter, we'll be looking at some of the ways you can use PowerShell to automate some of your admin tasks on all your active devices. Whenever you need to perform a task, you should ask yourself these two questions:

- How often will this task have to be performed?
- How long will it take me to do this task manually?

When you have the answers to those questions, you have the answer as to whether that task should be scripted in PowerShell.

When we start, it is likely that we will do all our PowerShell tasks as individual units. What that means is that, whenever a script is performed as a series of instructions, we have to wait until the task is returned before interacting further with the console.

However, getting around this is quite simple; all you need to do is start another console to get a new instruction under way while the first is finishing up. But, while that works okay, it isn't an ideal situation, and it certainly isn't an efficient way for system admins to do their work, for the following reasons:

- First, you cannot transmit the variable values from one console to another

- Second, you also can't easily pass the results between consoles
- Third, it isn't possible to individually identify the processes on each separate console.

Let's take a simple example. Tomorrow morning you go to work. When you reach your work station, there is an email asking you to do one action on 30 servers. Are you really going to sit there and open up 30 separate consoles in PowerShell? Of course not.

There is a neat feature in PowerShell, designed to help you get around the problem of multiple consoles, and that feature is called jobs.

The Jobs

With jobs at your disposal, you can asynchronously perform scripts and background instructions, and there are several cmdlets (instructions) that can be applied to jobs:

CMDLET	Description	Module Name
Get-Job	List jobs	Microsoft.PowerShell.Core
Receive-Job	Get results from jobs	Microsoft.PowerShell.Core
Remove-Job	Delete jobs	Microsoft.PowerShell.Core
Resume-Job	Restart job	Microsoft.PowerShell.Core

Start-Job (1) Start job	Microsoft.PowerShell.Core
Stop-Job (2) Stop job	Microsoft.PowerShell.Core
Suspend-Job Interrupt job	Microsoft.PowerShell.Core
Wait-Job Wait for another action to end	Microsoft.PowerShell.Core

1) You cannot use this for remote instructions; Invoke-Command must be used.
2) You should not need to use this in normal time as jobs automatically stop once their actions are finished.

Jobs fall into several categories, namely:

- Background
- Remote
- Scheduled
- Workflow

Let's delve into these now

BackgroundJob

Let's look at the instruction below - lists your firewall's active rules and uses their direction to sort them by:

Show-NetfirewallRule| sort direction | ?enabled-eq"true" | ft-property @{label="Name" ; expression={$_.displayname}}, @{label="Direction" ; expression={$_.direction}}

So, here, we've used an instruction that has conditions, which will make the processing time a longer. Starting a job is simple – the previous instruction line is passed in a ScriptBlock to StartJob, and then GetJob is used to follow what happens with the job.

Start-Job -ScriptBlock{Show-NetfirewallRule| sort direction | ?enabled -eq"true" | ft-property @{label="Name" ; expression={$_.displayname}}, @{label="Direction" ; expression={$_.direction}}}

Get-Job

On the console, the output should contain:

- An 'ID' – this is unique
- A name – by default this will be of the syntax, "Job<ID>"
- The job type – a BackgroundJob in our case
- The position – Failed, Running or Completed
- An indication whether the data can be displayed
- The station the instruction was performed at
- The completed instruction

Receive-Job is used to procure the data.

NOTE - -Keep should be added to Receive-Job to recover the data, thus allowing you to retain the results once verified. If you don't do this, the job stays available, but the results are erased.

So, we can now get the firewall rules for our computer:

PS > Receive-Job -ID 2 -Keep

NOTE – Remember to delete a job once you have used it

PS > Remove-Job -ID <ID>

Really, we haven't done anything complex here but you should consider giving your jobs names just so they are more visible:

PS > Start-Job -Name <JobName>

RemoteJob

Systems administrators would benefit from automating their recurring tasks as much as they can. Often, they get asked to perform an action on multiple servers at the same time and to do so as quickly as possible. They know that time is of the essence and they have to find the best way to do the job quickly to minimize any potential disruption. It is for that reason Remote-Job was created – here's an example:

```
PS > Get
ItemPropertyHKLM:\SOFTWARE\Wow6432Node\Microsoft\
Windows\CurrentVe
```

```
sion\Uninstall\* | Select-Object
DisplayName,DisplayVersion,Publisher,InstallDate|
```

```
? {$_.DisplayName-ne $null} | sort DisplayName
```

The above instruction lists all the software on the computer, after searching the registry and retrieving the data. Note that the software is x64; for software x86 installations, you will find the settings at:

```
HKLM:\SOFTWARE\Microsoft\Windows\CurrentVersion\Uni
nstall\
```

There are a few possibilities for doing this:

1. You could start the job, using a connection to a remote computer using a -ScriptBlock, which would display the job on the workstation

   ```
   Start-Job -Scriptblock {Do something -ComputerName
   Server1}
   ```

2. You could start the job on a remote machine; the ScriptBlock instruction does work remotely but will display all the data on your workstation. The important

part here - -AsJob – ensures the job is done remotely using the -ComputerName parameter

Invoke-Command   -Scriptblock{Do   something}   - ComputerNameServer1 -AsJob

3. You could open a remote session on another machine. Anything done on a remote machine is the same as what is done locally, but is handled remotely.
    PS >Enter-PSSession-ComputerNameServer1[Server1]:
    PS > Start-Job -ScriptBlock{Do something}

PSScheduleJob

Onto the next stage. We now know how to use the jobs in PowerShell remotely and locally and you know about scheduled Windows tasks. Now we're going to schedule the PowerShell jobs, and there are two primary advantages to this:

• You can use cmdlets to manage planned tasks, meaning you can obtain the results from a scheduled job, for example, by using Receive-Job
• You can automatically create tasks in Windows Scheduler

In the next example, we will get all Windows services that have not yet been started but have an automatic mode configuration. This lets us check each morning to see if there have been any issues on a server.

PS >Get-wmiobject win32_service -Filter "startmode = 'Auto' AND state != 'running' " | select name, startname

To make things more visible, we've used a ScriptBlock variable (a temporary one) to store the instruction. Register-ScheduledJob is used, and the job is given a name:

PS >$checkService = {Get-wmiobject win32_service -Filter "startmode = 'Auto' AND state != 'running' " | select name, startname}

Register-ScheduledJob-ScriptBlock$checkService-Name 'Check Services'

NOTE – you must use Invoke-Command if you want a scheduled job created on a remote unit.

Right now, this job does not have a trigger. Triggers are used when we want the ScheduledJob run. The job is started on a set day and time or when a particular event happens, such as when the computer goes idle.

PS > Get-ScheduledJob-Id 1 | select Jobtriggers

JobTriggers-----------

{0}

The only action is a manual one, and in our case, we will plan it. Management of the triggers is done using these cmdlets:

CMDLET	Description	Module Name
Add-JobTrigger	Add Jobtrigger	PSScheduledJob
Disable-JobTrigger	Disable Jobtrigger	PSScheduledJob
Enable-JobTrigger	Enable Jobtrigger	PSScheduledJob
Get-JobTrigger	Get Jobtrigger	PSScheduledJob
New-JobTrigger	Create Jobtrigger	PSScheduledJob
Remove-JobTrigger	Delete Jobtrigger	PSScheduledJob
Set-JobTrigger	Set Jobtrigger	PSScheduledJob

First, the trigger is created and then stored in $daily trigger, which is temporary. That starts work at 7am, allowing all the information to come in ready for the daily check.

When we have created the trigger, the Add-JobTrigger cmdlet is used to link it to the last job.

$dailyTrigger= New-JobTrigger-Daily -At "07:00:00"

Add-JobTrigger-Name "Check Services" -Trigger $dailyTrigger

Get-ScheduledJob

What we want to do here is take a Get-ScheduledJob and process it to make sure it gets activated with the correct parameters. The trigger can always be disabled, if needed, using the Disable-JobTrigger cmdlet.

Get-ScheduledJob-name "Check Services" | Get-JobTrigger

Next, the Windows task scheduler is opened, and we check the PowerShell folder to make sure that the Check Services trigger has been created.

To end this brief discussion on triggers, it is worth noting that you can set a few advanced options. The parameter called Options is optional and below, you can see a complete example:

$dailyTrigger= New-JobTrigger-Daily -At "07:00:00"

$MyOptions= New-ScheduledJobOption-RunElevated

$checkService = {Get-wmiobject win32_service -Filter "startmode = 'Auto' AND state != 'running' " | select name, startname}

Register-ScheduledJob-ScriptBlock$checkService-Name 'Check Services'-ScheduledJobOption$MyOptions

Add-JobTrigger-Name "Check Services" -Trigger $dailyTrigger

Get-ScheduledJob

You can use any of these parameters if you want your Scheduled Job customized:

- -StartIfOnBatteries
- -StopIfGoingOnBatteries
- -WakeToRun
- -StartIfNotIdle
- -StopIfGoingOffIdle
- -RestartOnIdleResume
- -IdleDuration
- -IdleTimeout
- -ShowInTaskScheduler
- -RunElevated
- -RunWithoutNetwork
- -DoNotAllowDemandStart
- -MultipleInstancePolicy
- -JobDefinition

PSWorkflowJob

Last, we have the workflow jobs. Up to now, we have understood that we can use Jobs to ensure we can automate multiple tasks at the same time, but you can't do this with every system job. In the real world, systems have to deal with:

- The remote system you are working on restarts
- Tasks needing to be adjourned
- Bulk work needing to be processed, such as using Hyper-V to expand virtual stations, migrating the mailbox on the Exchange, and so on

So, how do we get around these? By using PowerShell workflows, which came in with PowerShell v3.0. Here, you can see a workflow, divulging simple info about your operating system:

```
workflow myfirstworkflow {     Get-CimInstance -ClassName
Win32_OperatingSystem | select Caption, Version}

myfirstworkflow
```

Do you know how to define a PowerShell function? Then you will easily grasp how workflows are defined. They have an identical structure; all you need is a keyword, Workflow, and a name.

Every command in that workflow is independent of the one that follows it. What that means is that no variable can be seen by any command – no data state is shared. Now, that seems somewhat restrictive, but you can do it by using a single condition – an InlineScript block. Then, PowerShell will see it as a single script in a one-off session:

```
Workflow DemoWFW {


    InlineScript {

        $var1 = Get-Host

        $version = $var1 | select version

        $version

    }


}
```


DemoWFW

You can also process PowerShell workflows as background jobs using the -AsJob parameter when the workflow asks for it:

PS > DemoWFW-AsJob-PSComputerNameServer1

```
Id   Name  PSJobTypeNameState        HasMoreDataLocation
Command

--   ----   ------------------  -------  ------------------ ---------  ---
-------

6  Job6  PSWorkflowJobRunningTrue     Server1  DemoWFW
```

Now, we should look at how to process commands simultaneously. We use the -Parallel keyword to process any tasks running in parallel and we're going to use a ForEach loop to process actions that are similar at the same time on each of the listed servers. This is a random process:

```
Workflow Get-SrvDiskDrive {

    $servers = "ADM01","ADM11"

    Foreach -Parallel ($srv in $servers) {

        Get-CimInstance  -PSComputerName  $srv  -ClassName
Win32_DiskDrive

    }

}
```

Get-SrvDiskDrive

The best way to see how activities are executed like this is to look at a simple diagram of a workflow. You can easily launch multiple commands at the same time and run a sequence of commands in parallel. You do this with the Sequence keyword, followed by a ScriptBlock containing the commands. The workflow will look much like the one below:

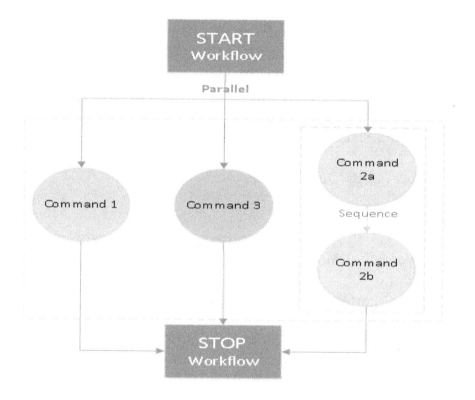

We can use the example below to illustrate this, showing a new employee arriving at your company:

Workflow Create-NewEmployee {

```
parallel {

  Create VM # Command 1

    sequence {

      Create AD account # Command 2a

      Create Mailbox # Command 2b

    }

  Create phone configuration  # Command 3

  }

}
```

Create-NewEmployee

You can choose to stop the workflow at any stage. If you want command processed at a certain time, SuspendWorkflow is used, and retrieving it requires you add the job ID to the Resume-Job cmdlet.

The Checkpoint-Workflow cmdlet offers something interesting – the ability to snapshot your workflow's current data. These show the variables and their values and the output. If an interruption to the workflow occurs and then the workflow starts again, the last snapshot saved is used and processing will start from them – if you didn't have checkpoints, your workflow would need to start all over again.

Below, you can see an example showing how the servers are backed up at the end of every processing:

```
Workflow  MyWorkflow {


    $variable = "Server1","Server2"

    Foreach -Parallel ($var in $variable) {

      # Do something ...

      Checkpoint-Workflow

    }

  }
```

MyWorkflow

Note that, when you do a CheckPoint, it does have an impact on the performance because data has to be collected and it has to be written to disk.

One important thing I do need to emphasize is that there is a difference between Checkpoint-Workflow and Suspend-Workflow. Where the latter pauses the current command, the former persists the workflow state at any given point in time by snapshotting the current state.

Creating a PowerShell workflow requires an XAML (eXtensible Application Markup Language) declarative workflow to be generated. The Windows Workflow Foundation will then use this for running the workflow. This code can be seen from the console as you can see in the next example. First, a workflow is created and then we look at the XAML representation:

```
Workflow Check-WinFeature {

        Get-WindowsFeature

    }

Check-WinFeature
```

To get this in XAML format:

PS > (Get-Command Check-WinFeature).XamlDefinition

And that brings us to the end of this chapter on automating administration tasks using PowerShell. We looked at how to use Jobs and Workflows to help you with routine tasks, and determined that one of the best ways for working out an implementation strategy for PowerShell tasks is a sequence of steps:

- Step One – Job
- Step Two – Workflow
- Step Three – Complex combinations, i.e. workflows within workflows

Creating PowerShell Jobs brings two primary benefits:

- Simple commands can run in the background – think command-line visibility
- You can see your Job results when you want to

Unless you are working with sensitive data, collecting results in one place makes managing remote background jobs much easier. Where sensitive data is concerned, you could keep the data on a remote computer to ensure its safety.

Workflow is incredibly flexible, and you can customize it to meet your own company requirements and, when you have activities that could be executed parallelly, you can simply add them to a Workflow. That is the real strength of PowerShell Workflows.

To finish this book, we'll take a brief look at PowerShell Remoting.

Chapter 6: PowerShell Remoting

With PowerShell Remoting, you can run your commands or access full sessions on a remote system. If you are familiar with SSH, a method of accessing a remote terminal on a different OS, then you'll grasp this quickly.

There are a few ways you can make a connection to a remote computer cmdlet. The systems can be in a different or the same domain, or even for PowerShell workgroups. Here we are going to focus on three things:

- The Inbuilt parameter
- The Invoke-Command
- Remotely executing the PSSession command

Inbuilt -ComputerName parameter.

Lots of PowerShell cmdlets provide support for the -ComputerName parameter. This is used to describe the names of the remote computers, i.e. the Get-Process, Get-Service and Get-WMIObject cmdlets, among others.

Here's an example.

For remote servers in the same domain, just add -ComputerName credentials:

Get-Service Spooler -ComputerName Test1-Win2k12

And the output is:

PS   C:\Users\Administrator>   Get-Service   Spooler   -
ComputerName Test1-Win2k12

Status   Name   DisplayName

------   ----   -----------

Running   Spooler   Print Spooler

Or if you want to use WMI to get the BIOS information off the
computer:

Get-WmiObject win32_bios -ComputerName Test1-win2k12

The output for this is:

PS   C:\Users\Administrator>   Get-WmiObject   win32_bios   -
ComputerName Test1-win2k12

SMBIOSBIOSVersion   :   6.00

Manufacturer   : Phoenix Technologies LTD

Name   : PhoenixBIOS 4.0 Release 6.0

SerialNumber   : VMware-56 4d 0d 7f 8a 7e f6 fa-f2 55 1d b6
a3 52 80 9f

Version   : INTEL – 6040000

However, for remote servers in different domains, you might see an authentication error message like this one:

PS C:\> Get-Service -ComputerName Test1-Win2k12

Get-Service : Cannot open Service Control Manager on computer 'Test1-

Win2k12'. This operation might require other privileges.

At line:1 char:1

   + Get-Service -ComputerName Test1-Win2k12

   + ~~~~~~

   + CategoryInfo   : NotSpecified: (:) [Get-

Service], InvalidOperationException

   + FullyQualifiedErrorId   :
System.InvalidOperationException,Microsoft.PowerShe

ll.Commands.GetServiceCommand

To get rid of the authentication issue, lots of the cmdlets provide support for the -Credential parameter, the destination server credentials. As an example, take the cmdlet called Copy-Item.

This contains the -Credential parameter, and the command will work if you pass the credentials for the remove server directly:

Copy-Item 'C:\Temp\Encoding Time.csv' -Destination \\Test1-Win2k12\C$\Temp -

Credential $creds

However, not all commands, like Get-Process, Get-Service, etc., have support for the -Credential parameter, so you will need to use the methods we talk about below.

Invoke-Command Method

This is one of the more convenient of all the methods for processing commands on remote computers. To remotely run the commands, a computer name and a script block are required:

Invoke-Command -ComputerName Test1-Win2k12 -
ScriptBlock{Get-Service Spooler}

PS   C:\Users\Administrator>   Invoke-Command   -
ComputerName Test1-Win2k12 -

ScriptBlock{Get-Service Spooler}

Status   Name   DisplayName   PSComputerName

------   ----   -----------   --------------

Running   Spooler   Print Spooler   Test1-Win2k12

Here, we have assumed that Test1-Win2k12 is in the same domain, so we don't need to add any more credentials for a remote server connection. If it were in a different workgroup or domain, you would need to add the -Credential parameter, which is supported by Invoke-Command. Here's an example:

$creds = Get-Credential

Invoke-Command -ComputerName Test2-Win2k12 - ScriptBlock{Get-Service Spooler} -

Credential $creds

Output

Status   Name   DisplayName   PSComputerName

------   ----   -----------   --------------

Running   Spooler   Print Spooler   Test2-Win2k12

The PSSession Method

The PSSession method gives you a choice – entering PSSession to run the command, or, using a session variable to store the session and passing that variable to allow the command to remotely run.

Enter-PSSession cmdlet

With the Enter-PSSession cmdlet, a direct connection to a domain is possible to connect all the computers, or you can use the -Credential parameter to provide the relevant credentials in the cmdlet for the computers in the different workgroup or domain.

For Domain-joined Computers

Enter-PSSession Test1-Win2k12

When the command is run with the computer name, you will see the computer name is in the front of the path. This tells you that you are in the Remote Shell and the command can be run.

The output from the above is:

PS C:\Users\Administrator> Enter-PSSession Test1-Win2k12

[Test1-Win2k12]:   PS
C:\Users\Administrator.LABDOMAIN\Documents>

[Test1-Win2k12]: PS
C:\Users\Administrator.LABDOMAIN\Documents> Get-Service

Spooler

Status   Name   DisplayName

------   ----   -----------

Running   Spooler   Print Spooler

If the computer is in another workgroup, the credentials must be passed in the cmdlet, like this:

Enter-PSSession Test2-Win2k12 -Credential (Get-Credential)

And the output is:

[Test2-Win2k12]:   PS   C:\Users\Administrator\Documents> Hostname

Test2-Win2k12

The Exit-PSSession command is used to end a session.

The Session Variable

The session variable can be used for remotely connecting to the server, and you will need the New-PSSession cmdlet with the name of the remote computer for this. That session needs to be stored in the variable which can then be used by the cmdlet that is supported, such as Enter-PSSession or Invoke-Command.

For example:

$sess = New-PSSession Test1-Win2k12

When you look at the $sess variable value, you will see it can be used for retrieving the cmdlet output on the Test1-Win2k12 machine:

Invoke-Command -Session $sess -ScriptBlock{Get-Service Spooler}

PS C:\Users\Administrator> Invoke-Command -Session $sess -ScriptBlock{Get-

Service Spooler}

Status   Name   DisplayName   PSComputerName

------   ----   -----------   --------------

Running   Spooler   Print Spooler   Test1-Win2k12

Conclusion

Thank you for taking the time to read this guide, "PowerShell: A Comprehensive Guide to Windows PowerShell," I hope that you found it useful.

Of course, there is much more to PowerShell than what I have written here but I have covered the basics of what you need to know. Scripts and cmdlets are the backbone of PowerShell and once you understand them and know how to write them, well, the world is your oyster.

Learning PowerShell means saving you time in administration tasks and money in staff hours having to do those tasks. Automate the everyday tasks and your time is freed up to concentrate on the big stuff!

This is just a stepping stone, a guide for you to refer to whenever you are unsure. Microsoft provides plenty of backup and system support and are one of the best resources for when things go wrong – make sure you use them.

Thank you once again for reading this and good luck on your PowerShell journey – once you use it, you will never look back.